IS GOD MAGIC?

**Enriching Discoveries About
Living in God's World**

by
Rexella Van Impe

All Scripture quotations are from the King James Version of the Bible.

Copyright © 1993 by Jack Van Impe Ministries

Printed in the United States of America.

Jack Van Impe Ministries
P.O. Box 7004 • Troy, Michigan 48007
In Canada:
Box 1717, Postal Station A
Windsor, Ontario N9A 6Y1

ISBN 0-934803-87-0

CONTENTS

1

Is God Magic?

A little boy asked his mother one day, "How can God love everybody? Is He magic?"

He couldn't understand how anyone—not even God—could love everyone. After all, there are so many of us, and some of us are so unlovable. To a child's way of thinking it would take nothing short of magic to be *that* loving.

You and I know that God is much more than magic. He's our all-powerful heavenly Father! In John 13:34,35, Jesus said to His disciples, *A new commandment I give unto you, That ye love one another; as I have loved you, that ye also love one another. By this shall all men know that ye are my disciples, if ye have love one to another.*

Jesus knew how unlovable people can be. He knew how unappreciative, unkind, thoughtless, selfish, quick to judge and criticize, and very mean we humans can act. Even within that intimate circle of the twelve disciples, there was envy, jealousy, and even murder. And these were the men upon whom Jesus was counting. The spread of the gospel depended upon the disciples showing love to each other and to others. So to these men, only a few short hours before His crucifixion, Jesus gave the supreme command, "Love one another." And it should be our number one priority today.

But that's just it. We don't love one another as we should. In fact, a good many of us Christians are downright unloving *much* of the time. So how do we get the love of God in our lives?

Where do we begin?

The place to begin is with the people around us—those in our homes, in our places of work, in our friendships, and in our churches. Someone has said we need "an observable love and openness." I like that. Love isn't love until it begins at home.

I heard of a woman whose husband was very outgoing, charming, and loving to everyone outside his home. But, often, to his family he was moody and irritable. He wasn't always outgoing, charming, and loving to them. In fact, his moodiness and his venting his anger and frustrations on his wife and children were destroying the love within his home.

One day in an effort to help him see what he was doing, his wife asked, "Honey, why don't you save some of your charm for us?" That took courage, but it helped.

Of course, we all need a place where we can let some steam off, let our hair down, and kick our shoes off and relax with those who will understand and not misjudge us. But there must be a balance whereby we also remember to show our love. Continual unloving mistreatment of those dearest to us will drive them away. I've heard such sad stories through the years of how people's hearts have become hard and cold because the love they once had for each other had not been nurtured.

Our example is Jesus. I'm sure He didn't always find it easy to show love. The Bible tells us that Jesus was tempted in all points as we are (see Hebrews 2:18). When the self-righteous Pharisees tried to trip Jesus up, it would have been easy for Him to withhold His love from those who were cruel, arrogant, and unjust. But Jesus never yielded to that temptation. He showed love in the most impossible of human situations. Jesus was love in action. He demonstrated His compassion over and over again in His dealings with those who desperately needed help, healing, and forgiveness.

Let love be your aim

The Apostle Paul gave the Corinthian Christians a goal that should be foremost in our minds as well. He said, "Let love be your aim" (see 1 Corinthians 14:1). Those words were preceded by the great love chapter in the Bible, 1 Corinthians 13. Those verses are so familiar to everyone, but perhaps their familiarity has dimmed their meaning. Let's look at them.

Though I speak with the tongues of men and of angels, and have not charity [love], I am become as sounding brass, or a tinkling cymbal.

And though I have the gift of prophecy, and understand all mysteries, and all knowledge; and though I have all faith, so that I could remove mountains, and have not [love], I am nothing.

And though I bestow all my goods to feed the poor, and though I give my body to be burned, and have not [love], it profiteth me nothing.

[Love] suffereth long, and is kind; [love] envieth not; [love] vaunteth not itself, is not puffed up,

Doth not behave itself unseemly, seeketh not her own, is not easily provoked, thinketh no evil;

Rejoiceth not in iniquity, but rejoiceth in the truth;

Beareth all things, believeth all things, hopeth all things, endureth all things.

[Love] never faileth: but whether there be prophecies, they shall fail; whether there be tongues, they shall cease; whether there be knowledge, it shall vanish away.

And now abideth faith, hope, [love], these three; but the greatest of these is [love] (1 Corinthians 13:1-8,13).

What a beautiful description of love! This chapter describes love in three ways—what it is, what it isn't, and what it does.

Love is:
- ♥ very patient and kind
- ♥ enduring, without weakening
- ♥ able to bear up under anything
- ♥ ready to believe the best of others

- ♥ loyal no matter the cost
- ♥ a growing thing—growing out of God's love for and in us.

Love is not:
- ♥ jealous or envious
- ♥ boastful or proud (inflated or puffed up with pride)
- ♥ conceited and arrogant
- ♥ touchy, fretful, or resentful
- ♥ rude and haughty
- ♥ possessive
- ♥ irritable or easily provoked
- ♥ selfish and self-seeking
- ♥ glad about injustice.

Love does:
- ♥ rejoice in the truth
- ♥ not hold grudges
- ♥ hardly notice when others do it wrong
- ♥ not demand its own way
- ♥ hope all things
- ♥ stand its ground in defending someone it loves
- ♥ not fail—does not fade out, become obsolete, or come to an end.

How loving are you?

Do you want to measure your "love level"? Here's an exercise that really works. Try substituting "I" in place of the word *love* in 1 Corinthians 13. Does it read right? Is that an accurate description of you? Can you honestly say, "I am very patient and kind. I am not easily provoked. I do not hold grudges"?

The Bible has so much to say about love. Here are some other verses to help us understand the nature of real love. First John 4:8 says, *He that loveth not knoweth not God; for God is love.* That verse says God is love. That is His nature. He is a heavenly Father who has divine compassion. And if we are His children, we must love, too—and not just those who love us, but even the unlovable. Jesus said, *Love your enemies, bless them that curse you, do good to them that hate you, and pray for them which despitefully use you, and persecute you; that ye may be the children of your Father which is in heaven...For if ye love them which love you, what reward have ye? do not even the publicans the same?...Be ye therefore perfect, even as your Father which is in heaven is perfect* (Matthew 5:44-46,48).

One day a so-called expert on Moses' law came to Jesus to test Him. He asked, *"Master, what shall I do to inherit eternal life?"*

Notice Jesus' reply: "You shall love the Lord your God with all your heart, and with all your soul, and with all your strength, and

11

with all your mind; and your neighbor as yourself."

The man, wanting to justify *his* lack of love for some people, asked, *"And who is my neighbor?"* (Luke 10:25-29).

You see, he was so much like us. He wanted to love the lovable, those who were easy to love. But Jesus said we are to love without discrimination, the way He loves us.

It's never too late

Perhaps you feel you've been so unloving in the past, that there is no way you can salvage your relationships. It's never too late with the help of the Lord. It may take time, but God can do a work of healing in your heart so that you genuinely love others. His Word to you is simply this: *Commit thy way unto the Lord; trust also in him; and he shall bring it to pass* (Psalm 37:5).

I want you to know that Jack and I love you. Our prayer is that you will learn to speak the truth in love and fully *grow up* in Christ (see Ephesians 4:15) so that the world will know that you, too, are one of Christ's disciples.

2
God's Love Letter

One of the nicest things about holiday seasons is being with our family and friends—having the privilege of sharing worship, food, and fellowship with those we love. Oh, how Jack and I cherish those blessed times with special people and, in particular, with one another.

Even when circumstances make it impossible to be together, we can get in touch by telephone or through the mail. We talk by phone with friends and loved ones all across the country...sometimes overseas.

We especially enjoy reading the many beautiful cards we receive from those special, thoughtful people who take time to express their love.

The other day I was going through some personal items I've saved over the last few years—news items and inspirational thoughts clipped from newspapers and magazines, cards and notes from family and friends...and a very special collection of love letters from my husband.

Jack and I have worked together in the ministry over the years, and haven't had to be apart very often. But on those occasions when I couldn't travel with him to a crusade or speaking engagement, he wrote me the most beautiful letters.

A wonderful reminder!

I'd read those letters over and over, hanging on every word. How wonderful to be reminded that he loved me, missed me, and was looking forward to having me with him again soon!

I cherished every one of those wonderful love letters. I still do. Over the years I've gone back and read them again many times, especially when I was feeling lonely, insecure, or discouraged. And each time my husband's loving words would lift my spirits and give me new strength.

Needless to say, although I cleaned out some of the accumulated "clutter" the other day, I kept those letters!

As much as I treasure my husband's letters to me, there's another love letter that is even more precious to me. It's the greatest love letter of all—God's Holy Word.

God sent this letter special delivery to me...to you...and to every single person in the world. It's all about love—what love is, how God loves us, and the great love gift He has given us.

For God so loved the world, that he gave his only begotten Son, that whosoever believeth in him should not perish, but have everlasting life. For God sent not his Son into the world to condemn the world; but that the world through him might be saved (John 3:16,17).

Sadly, too often this greatest love letter of all has been laid aside, unopened. The people who most need to know that God loves them haven't even read His letter.

Read God's letter

Some of those who have read it or heard about it at one time or another have forgotten its wonderful message. They need to go back and read God's love letter again. I can testify from personal experience that it is just as meaningful the second, third—twentieth—time you read it as it was the first time.

You see, we need to be reminded daily that we are loved. We need to see anew how valuable we are to God—that His love and mercy to us are new every morning.

What an unspeakable thrill to know that God loves us. We must hear it, relish it, think about it, enjoy it. We need to claim the blessing of salvation and His divine provision for our every need. We need to claim the blessing of knowing that He is preparing a place for us so that we can be with Him one day, face to face.

We should read and reread God's love letter to us because we need to be reminded of the wonderful gift of His love which we have received.

Give thanks...and share

In these last days we must make a special effort to express our appreciation for this great gift of love. Then we must enter anew into the spirit of love by doubling our efforts to share the old, old story of God's great love with others.

Don't wait—start immediately! Right now—today—get out your "Love Letter" from

God, your Bible, and discover—and share—
how much you are loved.

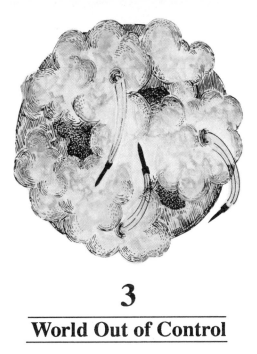

3

World Out of Control

During the war in the Persian Gulf, when Iraq's Saddam Hussein was aggressively defying the whole world and turning a deaf ear to any voice of reason, many people were confused and dismayed.

Even facing the mightiest air force and army in the world, this madman refused to back down. Instead, he provoked even further outrage by launching Scud missiles toward the peaceful neighborhoods of Israel and into Saudi Arabia.

"This is getting totally out of control," I heard one man say, shaking his head in frustration.

And a news commentator noted that after 40 years of East-West confrontation, just when the danger of the "cold war" finally seemed to be going away, the Persian Gulf exploded.

I think most of us often feel that we have very little control over what is happening in our world today.

Scientists warn that the ozone layer high in our atmosphere is being destroyed and the earth may soon become uninhabitable. In the meantime, our waste disposal systems can't handle all the trash and garbage our huge cities are piling up. Is our world out of control?

Economists tell us that most Americans work almost five months of the year just to pay their taxes, yet our federal deficit continues to soar...totally out of control.

Medical experts report that disease and suffering is still uncontrollable. New kinds of cancer are being found almost every year, and there is still no cure. AIDS, the modern plague, continues to take its deadly toll among increasing millions. In some parts of the world, entire populations are at risk.

Police officials admit they are losing the battle against crime in this country and the world. Murder, rape, robbery, and senseless violence make a mockery of our systems of so-called law and order. People don't feel safe going out on the streets—or even inside their own houses. Crime is out of control.

World political leaders have to acknowledge that after two major wars, hundreds of regional conflicts, and decades of work by an international organization dedicated to maintaining world harmony, we have not changed human nature or materially improved relationships between nations. The world's political turmoil seems more out of control than ever.

Is our world out of control?

At the very beginning of the war in the Persian Gulf, Jack and I were on national television with Paul and Jan Crouch. Much of the program was spent in prayer for our country, especially for the men and women on duty with our military forces. As Jan was praying, she said, "Oh, God, send a legion of angels to protect our troops!"

Instantly it went through my mind— *"They're already gone, Jan, because God says He knows what things we have need of before we ask Him, and that when we call on Him, He will answer"* (see Matthew 6:8; Psalm 91:15).

When it was my turn to lead in prayer, I asked the Lord to send His angels to protect the families our troops had left behind. I called on the Holy Spirit to comfort the little girls who had to go to bed each night without their mommies or daddies, and to strengthen the little boys who had to be the man of the house with dad away. And I had the comfort of knowing that even before I called out to Him, God was ready to answer.

"I am in control!"

Later, on the airplane flying home, I spent the travel time in prayer. And the Holy Spirit dealt with me in such a wonderful way. Again and again I sensed the voice of the Lord saying to me, "Rexella, I am in control! I have not left you ignorant—I've told you what's going to happen. Don't worry—I'm in control."

I began to realize that because of God's foreknowledge of what is going to happen, we must be ever vigilant in our prayer life to be in His perfect will. God provides answers for our prayers *beforehand*, according to His foreknowledge. When you pray, He already has the answer for your prayers—it's been ready since the dawn of creation, waiting for you to ask!

God's plan is working out

When circumstances seem totally unreasonable and unmanageable, the hand of God is at work behind the scenes. When everything in the whole world appears to be chaos from man's point of view, God can see the pieces of the puzzle falling into place according to His plan. He is in control. The Word of God is very plain about what will happen in this world. No matter what man does, God will still have His way.

Has He not spoken it? Shall He not bring it to pass?

How exciting to realize that you and I can be used of God to help bring about the fulfillment of His plan on the earth. When we see the world seemingly out of control, we have a powerful weapon at our disposal to bring about change and order! It's the weapon of loving, compassionate prayer!

God knows what is needed before we pray, and He's already prepared the answer. So if He can depend on you and me to ask, He's already prepared to take control of the situation.

Why we must pray

I believe if we fail to pray and ask God to send the answer for a particular situation, it may not be dispatched. There is great truth in the old song that says:

Oh, what peace we often forfeit,
Oh, what needless pain we bear,
All because we do not carry
Everything to God in prayer.

Look around your world today, my friend. Does it seem out of control? Is the confusion, strife, trouble, and pain more than you can handle alone? Try prayer!

When you cry out to Him, God will give you peace—a peace that is greater than just a temporary lull in the fighting, or a shaky, uncertain cessation of hostilities. He'll give you a peace that will surround you even in the midst of trouble.

Jesus said, *My peace I give unto you: not as the world giveth, give I unto you. Let not your heart be troubled, neither let it be afraid* (John 14:27).

Is the world out of control? As far as man is concerned—yes! But not for God. He's in control!

I pray that God will open our spiritual eyes today and let us see the "long" view. And as the fog of doubt and confusion rolls away, we'll be able to see the glorious truth expressed so well in the simple eloquence of the old Negro spiritual that says:

HE'S GOT THE WHOLE WORLD IN HIS HANDS!

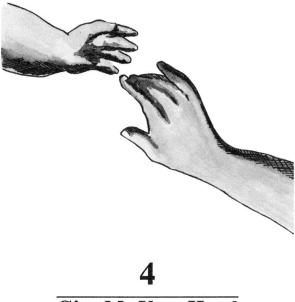

4

Give Me Your Hand

In my daily Bible reading, I've been noticing how much is mentioned about the hands of our Lord. Again and again the Gospels relate how He reached out to people in their need and hurt and sorrow. And when He touched them, they were never the same again.

His hands healed the sick

After He began His earthly ministry, great multitudes thronged about Him wherever He went. Those who were sick, blind, and lame—even those marked for death with the curse of leprosy—came to Him seeking to be healed and made whole.

When the hands of Jesus touched them, pain and suffering ceased, diseases and infirmities were cured, and lives shattered and ruined by sickness were restored.

His hands fed the multitude

It was the hands of Jesus that fed the multitudes who followed Him out into the desert place to hear His words. When evening came, Christ's disciples urged Him to send the people away. But Jesus saw their hunger and weariness and, in compassion, desired to minister to them.

Taking a few small loaves and fishes—barely enough for one small boy's lunch—the Lord blessed the food. Then His hands began to break and divide the bread and fish into portions which He gave to His disciples to serve.

We're told that 5,000 men were fed that day, not counting the women and children. And when everybody had eaten all they wanted, there were twelve baskets full of leftovers! The hands of Jesus not only provided enough...but plenty to spare.

His hands blessed the children

Loving children as I do, my heart is

touched to read the biblical account of how the hands of Jesus blessed and comforted the little children. He specifically told His disciples not to prevent them from coming to Him. And in my mind's eye, I can see the Lord sitting down and opening His arms to them. As they eagerly jostled about, perhaps He lifted a toddler into His lap, shook hands with an older lad, touched the cheek of a shy little girl. And as His gentle hands patted little shoulders and smoothed tousled hair, the Lord blessed these little ones. Somehow I think they probably never forgot that day when the hands of Jesus touched them.

The hands of the Master

No doubt the hands of Jesus were strong and powerful. Growing up around Joseph's carpenter shop, He probably learned to hold and use various tools to shape and assemble wood into useful items. His hands knew how to work.

It was those strong hands that later would grasp a whip as an indignant Jesus drove the callous moneychangers out of the holy halls of the Temple. Those hands were instruments of righteousness and justice.

It was those hands that reached out to lift and save impetuous Peter who, after walking on the water toward Jesus, took his eyes off the Lord and began to sink.

There are so many other references to the hands of Jesus that we could talk about. But the single most important mention of Christ's hands is when they were nailed to the cross.

A very dear, life-long friend gave me a beautiful wall plaque, which I have hanging in my kitchen. It says:

> I asked Jesus, "How much do You love me?"
> "This much," He answered, and He stretched out His arms and died.

Greater love hath no man than this, said Jesus, *that a man lay down his life for his friends* (John 15:13).

And who is Jesus' friend? The deeply spiritual and very religious? The learned and respectable? The proud traditionalists?

No, our Lord said that He was called *a friend of...sinners!* (Luke 7:34).

The Apostle Paul reminds us that *Christ died for the ungodly...in that, while we were yet sinners, Christ died for us* (Romans 5:6,8).

It is strangely and beautifully significant that the first person to benefit from Christ's sacrifice at Calvary was a thief on the cross next to His! Think of it—the first person to whom the Lord stretched out His nail-pierced hands was someone totally unworthy of His love.

Love-scarred hands

Some time ago my husband, Jack, and I were guests at a Christian fellowship dinner in another city. During the meal I got acquainted and talked with a dear little mother who sat next to me. After a while, with tears streaming down her cheeks, she leaned over and whispered the sad story of a wayward daughter who had run away from home, mounted up many debts, and fallen to the very depths of sin, even into a life of prostitution.

"I pray for her every day," she said, "and every time I hear from her I beg her to come home. My husband doesn't make a lot of money, so I got a job to help pay off the debts our daughter made. I'm doing everything I know how to do to help her. Please pray with me."

When I reached out to take hold of this precious mother's hands to comfort her, they were rough and callused, scarred by long hours of hard work, week after month after year. Those hands were scarred by love...by a mother's selfless sacrifice and desperate desire to reach and save her wayward daughter.

As I held those hands and prayed, I was reminded of Christ's nail-scarred hands that also were pierced for that lost daughter...and for every lost sinner in the whole world. They were scarred for me...and for you!

Just as the hands of our Lord ministered to men and women, boys and girls, wherever He went during His time on earth, so we today can feel the touch of His hands in our daily lives. His power is still available to us today.

In our times of pain and suffering, He is still the Great Physician who lays His hands upon us and restores our bodies. Whether our healing comes through medication, the skill of a surgeon, or by the power of faith alone, we know that He is the source of all healing.

When we are hungry and experiencing a lack of supply—when we're empty physically, emotionally, and spiritually—Christ's hands will bless and multiply the smallest things we have to offer Him and make it sufficient to meet our need...with plenty to spare.

When we've tried and failed—when like Peter, we're sinking into the depths of trials and tribulations, with no hope in sight—He will come to us, walking on the waters of our stormy sea. His hand will save us, lift us up, and lead us safely to the solid rock!

The challenge of Easter

I love Spring! There's something special about seeing the sun light up winter's gray skies, and nature stir the grass and trees into new life. Surely it is no coincidence that we celebrate Easter in the Springtime.

Each Easter we are reminded that Christ died for us—but He rose again! Without Easter, we might be tempted to forget that it is through the outstretched arms and nail-pierced hands of Jesus that we have life eternal. Had it not been for His sacrifice on Calvary and His bodily resurrection, there would be no everlasting life.

As we look around us and see all of nature coming back to life anew, let us be reminded of Christ's great love for us.

But let us also be challenged to reach out in His love into every man's world with a helping hand. Let us emulate our Lord's great example and use the resurrection power that flows through us to minister to the needs of those around us.

Never forget that for many people in the world, their first glimpse of Christ may be in you...the only hands that will touch them in love, that will comfort, lift, and bless them, may be your hands.

Reach out whenever you can, wherever you can, to whomever you can. However unlovely or unworthy the person you find may be, remember that Christ's sacrifice is sufficient...and that He loves that individual just as much as He loves you.

Do not be afraid to stretch forth your hand to anybody. For you minister, not in your own strength and ability, but in His love. So when you reach out, it will not be just your hand that touches them, but the hand of God through you!

I love the beautiful gospel chorus that cries out—

Oh, to be His hand extended,
 Reaching out to the oppressed,
Let me touch Him, let me touch Jesus,
 So that others may know and be blessed.

Look around you today and find someone who is hurting or needy, someone who is in trouble. Ask God to guide you to someone who needs Jesus.

When you find them, don't hesitate or delay. Go to them with a smile filled with the light of His love and simply say...

"Give me your hand."

5

Someone With Skin On

I suppose this story has been told in a variety of ways, but it illustrates so well the heart-cry of all mankind.

As I heard it, a little boy woke up in the midst of a violent storm, frightened by the thunder and lightning, and cried out for his mother. She reassured him, and told him never to be afraid of the dark or the storm because God was right there with him.

In a few minutes the child cried out again, and the mother went back to his side and reminded the youngster of her earlier assurance that God was with him in the storm. "I know," said the lad, "but I want someone with skin on!"

Don't we all? Religions based on noble thoughts or impersonal cosmic forces, or centered around idols made of stone or wood, do not satisfy the deep longing inside the human breast for a God with whom we can have a personal, living experience. We seek a God we can touch—Someone with skin on—to be our Example, our Saviour, and our Intercessor.

Centuries after the time when God himself came down to the Garden of Eden in the cool of the evening to walk, talk, and have fellowship with Adam and Eve, sinful man had lost sight of who God was and what He was like. Mankind stumbled about in the dark, disobedient and lost.

So God sent His Son to earth once again to reveal to man what God is like and to restore the lines of communication and fellowship. And to help man relate to God, the Father wrapped His Christmas present to the world— the divine spirit and person of His Son—in human skin!

The Apostle Paul wrote, *For God, who commanded the light to shine out of darkness, hath shined in our hearts, to give the light of the knowledge of the glory of God in the face of Jesus Christ* (2 Corinthians 4:6).

Jesus, our Example

The old gospel song, "Where He Leads I'll Follow," has a tremendous message in its lyrics. One line in particular describes Jesus by saying, "He the Great Example is, and Pattern for me."

The truth is, Jesus gave us an example for *living* as well as His life. When we see how Jesus lived, how He acted, how He responded to other people and the circumstances of daily life, we catch a glimpse of how we should live. Oh, if only we would ask ourselves, "What would Jesus do?" when faced with life's tough decisions and choices.

We know that His life was an outpouring of love and joy. His very first recorded miracle was performed at a wedding! He had dear, cherished friends in Mary, Martha, and Lazarus, in whose home He enjoyed rest and fellowship. When Lazarus died and Jesus was called, we're told He wept for His friend. Onlookers even noted, *Behold how he loved him!* (John 11:36). And Jesus raised Lazarus from the dead.

The Gospels are filled with examples of the compassion of our Lord. *And Jesus, when he came out, saw much people, and was moved with compassion toward them* (Mark 6:34). We're told He taught them...and later fed them.

Acts 10:38 tells *how God anointed Jesus of Nazareth with the Holy Ghost and with power: who went about doing good, and healing all that were oppressed of the devil; for God was with him.*

This is the example Jesus set for us—He went about doing good. In love and compassion, He met people's needs, touching, healing, and lifting them. And that is what we are to do.

In today's dark world, you and I may well be the only light some people will ever see. We are the only hands of God that will ever touch them. Ours are the only feet that will bring the good news of the gospel to them.

I tell you, if Christ's hands are not extended through ours, His will never reach out to some people. That individual in your world crying out for someone with skin on to come to him...is waiting for you.

"Oh, Rexella," you say, "how could we ever expect to be like Jesus and minister as He did?"

Because He said so. Jesus said, *Verily, verily,* [truly, truly] *I say unto you, He that believeth on me, the works that I do shall he do also; and greater works than these shall he do; because I go unto my Father. And whatsoever ye shall ask in my name, that will I do,*

that the Father may be glorified in the Son
(John 14:12,13).

Jesus, our Saviour

A short time after the birth of Jesus, Mary and Joseph brought Him to Jerusalem to the Temple to be presented to the Lord, according to the law of Moses. Two remarkable and beautiful things happened there that day.

First, there was a priest named Simeon, an old man who had been promised that he would not die until he had seen the Lord's Christ. When He saw Jesus, he took Him in his arms, and blessed God, and said, *Lord, now lettest thou thy servant depart in peace, according to thy word: for mine eyes have seen thy salvation* (Luke 2:29,30).

There was also an 84-year-old prophetess named Anna in the Temple. The Bible says that *she coming in that instant gave thanks likewise unto the Lord, and spake of him* [Jesus] *to all them that looked for redemption in Jerusalem* (Luke 2:38).

Why is it so significant that Simeon and Anna recognized Jesus as the Saviour? Perhaps God knew that we today needed to see this confirmation of the faith of others in the holy Scriptures. The majority then and now could not see who He was and is because of spiritual blindness. The Lord Jesus entered the world He had created to rescue fallen man, yet those with whom He desired to be intimately associated rejected Him.

The Bible says, *He was in the world, and the world was made by him, and the world knew him not. He came unto his own, and his own received him not* (John 1:10,11).

Jesus knew the price He would have to pay as the Saviour of the world. The Christmas card picture of Him being revered as a beautiful baby in a manger was for a brief moment. The adulation of those touched by the compassionate prophet, teacher, and healer lasted only a few days.

Jesus grew up in a humble home, in a despised village. His brothers and sisters misunderstood Him. The religious leaders of the day hated Him. And finally, when He was falsely convicted and crucified, His own disciples forsook Him.

But He died for everyone to redeem all mankind, willingly, by choice. He came to be *a Saviour, which is Christ the Lord* (Luke 2:11).

Someone has said that Jesus would have come to earth, suffered and died, to save just one person. And I believe that is true. But it is also true that, had the Lord been born ten thousand times in Bethlehem, it would have been ineffective...unless He had a birth in our hearts. Only then is He our Saviour.

Jesus, our Intercessor

I've often heard the old folk proverb which suggests that before one criticizes a person, he should walk a mile in his shoes. The point is, of course, that one cannot really understand someone else's behavior unless one has gone through their tests and trials.

The writer of the Book of Hebrews reminds us that because Jesus, the Son of God, came down and wrapped himself in human skin and walked in our shoes, He knows what we're going through...He understands. *For we have not an high priest which cannot be touched with the feeling of our infirmities; but was in all points tempted like as we are, yet without sin* (Hebrews 4:15).

Under the law of Moses, the role of the high priest was to intercede before God for mankind. And Jesus, who provided the ultimate sin offering in His death on the cross, now serves as our Intercessor in heaven before the Father.

Having walked the rocky road of human existence before us, He fully understands what it means to be hungry, tired, and penniless ...to be misunderstood, slandered, falsely accused...to endure heartache, physical pain and suffering...even death!

Oh, He knows what you're going through, He understands what you need...and He cares! He sees your struggles, He hears your cry. And He is reaching out to you.

I heard about a little girl whose mother was in the hospital, and who was spending the night alone with her father. Soon after her dad turned out the lights, the little girl said, "Daddy, are you there?"

"Yes, child," he said, "I'm here."

It was quiet for a moment, and then a little voice asked, "Daddy, are you looking at me?"

What a joy to know that, in our darkest hours, we can go ahead and go to sleep knowing that Jesus stays awake all night looking after us!

I love the beautiful words of the old song that says,

Can we find a friend so faithful,
Who will all our sorrows share;
Jesus knows our every weakness;
Take it to the Lord in prayer.

Just now, reach out and touch the "skin" of Jesus the Lord, God's "unspeakable gift" of love. Receive Him as your Example, accept Him as your Saviour, trust Him as your Intercessor.

6

The Tragic Problem of Child Abuse

My husband and I were recently in Israel. Almost everywhere we went, we saw children, running, playing, shouting. I thought that Jesus must have seen children, too, as He visited the places we did, and I was tenderly reminded of how much He loves children.

On one occasion the disciples tried to keep the children from Jesus, and the Bible says He rebuked them. *Jesus said, Suffer little children, and forbid them not, to come unto me: for of such is the kingdom of heaven* (Matthew 19:14).

43

Jesus not only had a special love for children while He was here on earth, but when He returns He is going to give special attention to them. Zechariah 8:5 says, *And the streets of the city shall be full of boys and girls playing in the streets thereof.*

Unfortunately, there are people today who do not share God's love for children. Instead, they abuse children, mistreat them, and even kill them. Child abuse is now being called "the most under-reported crime in the United States." America's children—our nation's most precious resource—are in peril.

Scarcely a day goes by without the headlines screaming out the tragic loss of a child's life somewhere in the country, or the media reports another case of sexual abuse of an innocent child or the beating of a youngster. It is a tragedy, a crime of monstrous proportions, with children—the most vulnerable members of our society—the targets of abuse.

Psychologists are now telling us that parents who physically or emotionally abuse their small children were reared in a similar manner. In view of this, child abuse is a matter we must make our concern. My reading has revealed that parents who batter their children, whether emotionally, physically, or a combination of both, say that is how they were raised. They say they don't know any other way to keep their kids in line. Thus the cycle of abuse continues from one generation to another.

Abuse often goes unrecognized

One tragedy of child abuse is that parental or adult child abusers often go unrecognized for a number of reasons. Often the outside world really doesn't want to become involved in what could turn out to be a long, drawn-out situation. There may not be enough evidence for outsiders to justify their *early* involvement, or they may want to spare the child any additional, needless hurt.

Another reason child abusers go unrecognized and unpunished is because of adult denial. When a child reports that he has been or is being abused by an adult, too often his parents or the authorities will deny it. Some parents who do not wish to cause problems within the family or with friends or neighbors will shame their children into silence.

We have Sigmund Freud to blame, in part, for parental denial. He fashioned what came to be called the "seduction theory" based upon early encounters with young girls who were brought to him by their parents. In 1905 he published the theory that children were ruled by their infantile sexual desires and that the sexual "abuses" children reported could not be believed as real events because the abuses were merely the children's own deepest wishes.

Because of this, our culture, pervaded with Freudian psychology, for 60 years has ignored or de-emphasized children's reports of seduction, cruelty, and sexual coercion by family members and/or by friends or neighbors.

Some adults are now speaking out after years of silence and telling of their experiences as abused children. They say that a common message they received was, "You're bad even to think such thoughts," when they tried telling their mothers what was actually happening.

Fortunately, today people are beginning to be aware of child abuse, to talk about it, and to do something about it. Recent reports in the news media about child abuse at preschools have done much to heighten public awareness of the problem. This has led to the formation of community services and self-help groups to deal with the increasing problems both for abusers and the abused.

Awareness within the Christian community has grown along with public awareness. Adult "care-givers" in both arenas are working diligently to provide treatment and counsel. They are even teaching youngsters how to protect themselves from abuse and where to

46

go for help if it is needed. We should recognize and admit that the abuse of children is a problem that affects not only society but the church as well. The church should be ready at all times to minister to an abused child or to an abusive family.

What is child abuse?

How is child abuse actually defined? The public is, by and large, uncertain as to what constitutes abuse, and that accounts, in part, for an under-reporting of suspected child abuse.

"Doesn't every parent have the responsibility and the right to discipline his child?" someone may ask. As Christians, we believe we have a biblical mandate to train up our children in the way they should go and where necessary to use corrective measures. My own parents, as well as Jack's parents, exercised controlled discipline with us, and I see others doing the same. The key word is *controlled.*

Professionals who speak of child abuse are not referring to the spankings parents give to their children now and then when the children deserve a firm hand on the bottom of their anatomy. Abuse, they say, isn't something that happens "now and then." It is consistent and severe and is motivated by the parents'

47

hostility and unresolved inner conflict rather than by a desire to change the child's behavior. It is usually irrational and *uncontrolled*.

Often the abusing parent has unrealistic expectations of what the child is capable of doing and giving. I've seen parents fly into a rage in a restaurant when their two- or three-year-old spills his milk. Parents who respond in an uncontrolled manner will view the child's accident as a commentary on their behavior rather than as a normal three-year-old's clumsiness.

The National Committee for Prevention of Child Abuse describes child abuse in this way:

- Child abuse is an injury or a pattern of injuries to a child that is non-accidental.
- Child abuse is damage to a child for which there is no reasonable explanation.
- Child abuse includes nonaccidental physical injury, sexual molestation, neglect, and emotional abuse.

Nonaccidental physical injury may include severe beatings, burns, human bites, or immersion in scalding water.

Sexual molestation is exploitation of a child for the sexual gratification of an adult, such as rape, incest, fondling of the genitals, or exhibitionism.

Neglect is a failure to provide a child with the basic necessities of life which include food, clothing, shelter, or medical care.

Emotional abuse is excessive, aggressive, or unreasonable parental behavior that places unreasonable demands upon the child to perform above his capabilities. Examples may include constant teasing, belittling, or verbal attacks; no love, no support, and no guidance.

● Child abuse is NOT usually a single physical attack or a single act of deprivation or molestation. Child abuse is a *pattern of behavior.* Its effects are cumulative: the longer it continues, the more serious it becomes and the more serious the child's injuries.

Signs of abuse: what to look for

What should you look for if you suspect abuse? Are there signs?

Victims will often retreat into a silent world. The reason for this is that they are frightened or they may innately sense that what has happened to them is wrong and they are too embarrassed to tell. They believe they will be thought of as bad and that they will be blamed or punished.

Watch for physical signs, warnings that something is amiss. There may be bruises, welts, genital pain, or bleeding. If a parent observes drastic changes in a child's behavior, he or she should be sensitive to the fact that something may be wrong. A toilet trained child may suddenly, for no apparent reason, become a bed wetter. A child might resist a babysitter whom he or she hadn't objected to previously.

Children may be sending unspoken messages—an unusual quietness...not wanting to discuss things that are happening at school. Or the children may be unusually fearful. There may be a cringing, drawing back from being touched, a reluctance to meet strangers or even people they know.

A child's inability to concentrate in school and subsequent poor grades may indicate that some form of abuse is occurring in the home. A child's withdrawal from friends and fun activities or difficulty in sleeping or eating are other signs that something is amiss.

What can you do?

If you are a parent or care-giver and you suspect child abuse, take the child to a physician. Reassure the child that you love him, but take steps to protect the child by calling the police or child welfare bureau. Above all, provide that assurance the child needs from you. Impress upon him that he didn't do anything wrong in telling you. If you suspect your spouse is molesting your child, win the child's confidence and ask appropriate questions.

Teach your children how to recognize danger. Let them know that most adults are loving people but that there are some who may cause them harm. They need to be taught that they are not to go anywhere with a stranger or even with a casual acquaintance and that they are never to accept candy or money from such a person. Teach your children to say no to an adult who tries to bribe them in some way.

Teach your children that there are some parts of the body that are not to be touched by other people. You can teach your children that not even people they love and trust should ever touch them in these places...and they should be wary when adult friends are acting secretive or when they say, "Don't tell."

If you are an abusive parent who needs help, I am happy to tell you that there are support systems available. Parents Anonymous has chapters throughout the country which offer non-judgmental help. Their toll-free number is 1-800-421-0353. Another self-help organization is called SCAN, Stop Child Abuse Now. For these and other helpful groups, look in your telephone book under "Child Abuse."

There are also community mental health clinics which provide help; family counseling services; city, county, or state social agencies; family mediation and crisis centers; and parents' aid societies. All such agencies and organizations are listed in the telephone directory white or yellow pages and most provide services free of charge.

If you suspect that a child is being abused in some way—whether physically, verbally, emotionally, sexually, or through neglect—act at once by calling the police department. Even if you have no proof, don't hold back. Don't be afraid of "causing trouble." I've been told that the police will act on anonymous complaints of suspected child abusers, so don't fear involvement with the authorities. Remember, it is the lives of innocent children who are in peril.

* This chapter is an excerpt from Rexella Van Impe's book, *Beware: Children in Peril.*

7

Seeing America ~~Through~~ Without Rose-Colored Glasses

Not long ago Dr. Van Impe and I were having dinner in a little restaurant near our home. As we were eating, a friend of ours came in with her little granddaughter for their evening meal.

The little girl ran up to me and exclaimed, "Oh, Mrs. Van Impe, see my new sunglasses! They make everything look so pretty."

I had to smile at her childish exuberance. And after our darling little friend went with her grandmother to their own table, I exclaimed to my husband, "No wonder everything appears so pretty to her—she's looking through rose-colored glasses!"

Each year we celebrate the birth of the United States and our nation's independence. As we gratefully consider the blessings and benefits of living in our great land, it's easy to allow our view of America to be colored just a bit too rosy.

Having traveled in 50 countries around the world, I must say that each time I return to my beloved homeland I am tempted to look at America through rose-colored glasses. At times I've actually had to restrain myself from running from the plane and kissing the ground, as I thanked God for America.

But I recognize that my country has some alarming faults and problems. While the United States may seem to be in great shape when compared to all the other countries in the world, when we measure ourselves against God's standard there is much cause for concern.

It seems to me there has been too much compromising—too much relaxation among all our citizens.

We've relaxed our attitude toward hard work and doing our best. We've lowered our standards of excellence and discarded our pride of accomplishment.

Do you ever feel that American workers are more interested in time off and leisure activities than in the quantity and quality of the work they do? Someone has said the prevailing attitude now seems to be, "Don't put yourself out—that's good enough."

And while most Americans are still generous and helpful to people suffering need or calamity, there is a growing tendency to look the other way and say, "It's none of my business" or "I don't want to get involved."

I'm also concerned that our society—in the name of tolerance and individual liberty—has stood by and let our community standards of decency, morality, and ethics be trampled underfoot by vulgar, unscrupulous, and dishonest men. When will we learn there is no virtue in failing to stand up for what we believe? There is no right way to do the wrong thing!

It's time for us to wake up, rise up, speak up! It's time to take off our rose-colored glasses and look at our nation, our neighborhood, and our home in the cold, clear light of day. It's time to start seeing ourselves through God's eyes—the way he sees us!

How can we make America better? I believe with all my heart we must stop waiting for someone else to take action and do what we can, where we are! After all, a nation is people, and we can influence people. We can win them, lead them, guide them. And the best way to accomplish that is by our own personal example.

Be a Christian example of a good citizen

The Apostle Paul urged: *Be thou an example of the believers, in word, in conversation, in charity, in spirit, in faith, in purity* (1 Timothy 4:12).

That verse doesn't need much explaining, does it? Our very word, deed, and attitude must be Christ-like and set a leadership pattern that will inspire those around us. Paul went on to say in verse 16, *For in doing this thou shalt both save thyself, and them that hear thee*.

The thirteenth chapter of Romans deals with our Christian duty to the state and the duties of citizenship. We are instructed to obey the government and the laws of the land, and to pay our taxes.

As Christians, we should pray about everything that touches our lives and others. Our desire should always be for God's will to be done. I believe we should pray for those in authority over us, including our President, and state and local officials.

By being good Christians in our daily walk, we really can make America a better and stronger nation.

Get involved in the issues that shape America

Throughout the Bible, God expected His people to be involved in their country. When a nation was threatened by an enemy force, the king himself led the army. The citizens made up the ranks, or supplied needed provisions...then honored the heroes and celebrated the victory!

It's time we as Christians get more involved in every aspect of our country. It is right that we let our voices be heard on matters concerning religious freedom. But we must also be interested and actively involved in the social, moral, and political issues affecting America.

I'm tired of hearing people say contemptuously, "Politics is a dirty business and I don't want to have anything to do with it. After all, sooner or later all politicians turn out to be crooks." Almost always you'll find that those people never attend a public hearing or forum, never support a particular cause or candidate, fail to learn the facts about important issues (often believing and spreading untruths)—and perhaps seldom vote...unless it's **against** something or somebody.

I've had the privilege of getting personally acquainted with many elected officials, from the federal government in Washington, D.C., on down to the local level. I've discovered that there are many, many dedicated, honest, and hardworking public servants. One of their greatest concerns is that citizens too often are not interested in what goes on in government, and not enough of them get involved.

No matter what the cynics say, what you think and what you do does make a difference. You can help change things. Your voice is heard.

The Word of God commands us to *abhor that which is evil; cleave to that which is good* (Romans 12:9). I believe this requires more than lip service. We must get off the sidelines and into the mainstream. It's time to stop saying, "Somebody ought to do something," and start doing it!

If you share my concern about the devastating impact of abortion on the very soul of our country, I urge you to get involved. While we should never resort to violence, destruction, or other illegal acts as some misguided protesters have done, we can and should speak out at every opportunity. Perhaps you can help in a pro-life clinic, or actually provide support and assistance to a pregnant girl who otherwise might feel she had no choice but abortion.

Recently I heard about a group of citizens in Oklahoma who were concerned about the blatant pornography being openly displayed in convenience stores before the curious eyes of children. They spoke out against it! So effective were their efforts that one chain of stores removed the offensive magazines from its shelves altogether, others moved them behind the counter, out of sight—and the city government began drafting an ordinance to control the display and sale of sexually-oriented publications.

In thousands of schools, businesses, churches, and homes across our nation, multitudes of people have gotten involved in a grass roots effort to help the starving millions in Ethiopia and other famine-stricken African countries. One school in New York received national attention when its students (all from poor or low income homes) raised several hundred thousand dollars to buy and transport food to Africa. Their example inspired similar efforts in communities from coast to coast.

Involvement is tremendously fulfilling personally—and it gets things done. Look around you for what needs to be done...and set out to do it!

Let's have revival!

I love to read about the impact some of the great men of God had upon our country in their day. The record shows that when spiritual giants like Whitefield, Wesley, Finney, and a host of others conducted their great revivals in America, they closed down the saloons, and crime decreased.

Now we often have so-called evangelistic meetings that have almost no impact—some church members aren't even aware there is a meeting going on!

Our nation needs a revival of old-fashioned, Bible-based, life-changing salvation, and faith in God. The people of the United States need a renewed appreciation for God's goodness and an increased awareness of their dependence upon Him.

You and I must be part of a new emphasis on evangelism and the Church, on winning people to Christ. The more people we get to accept the Lord Jesus, the better our country is going to be.

We must start where we are—in our house, our neighborhood, our community. Perhaps it is true that we personally cannot reach the entire world—but we can reach **our** world.

I love that beautiful song that expresses the prayer, "Let there be peace on earth, and let it begin with me." Each of us can adapt that prayer and cry out, "Let there be revival in America, and let it start in my house...in my heart."

Oh, may we love our country and its people in a real, practical way, like we've never loved before. Let's take off our rose-colored glasses and see America as God sees it. Let's allow Him to wash our eyes with tears of repentance and intercession.

Let's join hands across this nation and work together for Christ until we make our country God's country!

8

Were You There?

One of my favorite songs often heard at Easter time is the beautiful old black spiritual, "Were You There?" The simple but haunting words of this great classic remind us of the suffering and sacrifice of our Lord at Calvary, as well as the triumphant victory of His Resurrection.

Because Christ suffered and died—not for His own sins but for yours and mine—in a very real sense we were there at Golgotha on that awesome day of destiny nearly 2,000 years ago. And it is important that we remind ourselves of what happened there—of the death that gave us life...of the penalty paid that set us free.

Were you there at the place of the skull which became the place of life everlasting?

Dr. Van Impe and I have gone to the outer edge of the old city of Jerusalem to Golgotha, the place of the skull, to view the place where Jesus died for us. Perhaps it is only fitting that today there is an ancient cemetery on top of this rugged, rocky hill. And sure enough, when viewed from below at enough distance for good perception, the shape of Mt. Calvary is much like a human skull!

When I was there, the ugly reality of what really happened to Jesus on that spot struck me. He was tortured, maimed, and killed there. He was mocked and humiliated, then nailed to a rough-hewn cross. His blood poured out and stained the wood, the rocks, and the ground.

Not long ago a friend of mine asked, "But why did Jesus have to die?" The answer is clear—mankind sinned, and the Bible says *the wages of sin is death* (Romans 6:23).

For centuries God allowed men to sacrifice the blood of animals as a temporary covering for their sins. This was an imperfect sacrifice, with limited efficacy. The blood of goats and calves could not take away sin (see Hebrews 10:4).

Only the sacrifice of Jesus Christ, the perfect, sinless, Son of God, was pure and holy enough to wash away the stain of sin for all mankind. No wonder John the Baptist, upon seeing Jesus, cried out, *Behold the Lamb of God, which taketh away the sin of the world* (John 1:29).

Because of Christ's willing sacrifice, the place of death became the place of life—yes, everlasting life—for all who receive the Lord.

Were you there for the noonday darkness where we received the Light of the world?

The gospels tell us that Christ was crucified at 9:00 a.m. and that from noon until 3:00 p.m., darkness covered the earth! Imagine the daylight hours as dark as midnight, when there was no light in the heavens and the sun refused to shine. When the "light of the world" was dying, darkness was everywhere!

Darkness symbolizes trouble and despair, fear and hopelessness. We've all gone through dark days when it seemed there was no way out of our desperate situation, and everything around us looked black. Jesus tasted of that awful darkness for us, when there was no joy or no hope. But in the midst of the darkest hour in all of human history, He brought new light!

How fitting that the Prophet Isaiah was anointed by the Spirit of God to look down the corridors of time to the coming of Jesus and proclaim, *The people that walked in darkness have seen a great light: they that dwell in the land of the shadow of death, upon them hath the light shined* (Isaiah 9:2).

Today the world seems dark again. I know people who don't even want to watch the news on TV or read the newspaper because everything looks so black and bleak. If ever we needed the light of the world, it's today. There's no other way out of the darkness. But if we follow Him, we can live in the joy of His sunshine in our lives.

Were you there at the place where Jesus said, "I thirst," and from which now comes living water?

One of the worst forms of human suffering is to be thirsty. I remember being in Israel while we were taping a TV special. On a blindingly bright, blistering hot day (120 degrees Fahrenheit), I was recording a song on a hill overlooking Masada. The sun beat down mercilessly, and the desert wind swirled the sand around us.

After a while I got so thirsty I could hardly speak, much less sing. My mouth was almost too dry to swallow—it felt like waves of desperation mounting until I was finally given something to drink.

I thought of Jesus hanging on a cross, after having been beaten with whips, crowned with cruel thorns, and nailed to the beams that suspended Him between heaven and earth. In the midst of the agony of crucifixion, He also was stricken with thirst.

When they offered Jesus a drink, He realized that it contained something to help dull the pain of His suffering—and He refused it. He allowed nothing to keep Him from experiencing the utter depths of the thirsty soul.

All of us have a thirst within that cannot be satisfied except by the Living Water of God. We may drink from the waters of pleasure and ambition, even taste the wine of riches and self-indulgence. But nothing earth has to offer can quench the thirsting of our souls.

Jesus said, *Whosoever drinketh of the water that I shall give him shall never thirst; but the water that I shall give him shall be in him a well of water springing up into everlasting life* (John 4:14).

Were you there for the weeping and sorrow which led to joy and blessings?

The cross of Calvary was a place of weeping and sorrow. The Bible says that women stood weeping at the foot of the cross. The disciples of Jesus were also overcome with sorrow. No doubt there were those who had been healed, taught, and blessed by the Lord who looked on that day. Their hearts must have been broken to see this Miracle Worker dying. And other followers who thought Jesus was to be Israel's new leader and deliverer must have been bitterly disappointed, too. "What's happening?" they cried. "We thought this was our Messiah!"

But if Jesus had not experienced such great sorrow, He would never have understood the sorrows of mankind. Isaiah prophesied, *He is despised and rejected of men; a man of sorrows, and acquainted with grief...surely he hath borne our griefs, and carried our sorrows* (Isaiah 53:3,4).

Because of His sacrifice, we know that all our tears will be wiped away and our sorrow replaced by divine joy. Thank God, the psalmist wrote, *Weeping may endure for a night, but joy cometh in the morning* (Psalm 30:5).

Were you there for the time of anguish which provides our comfort?

On Calvary, Jesus gave His body and soul as a sacrifice for us. He suffered unendurable sorrow and pain. Here He bore our sins. We cannot even imagine what it was like for the Perfect One, God in the flesh, to feel the defilement of every sin in the universe. Here was Jesus, who never did cheat, steal, lie, commit adultery, or do any other sin, suddenly burdened with the vileness and degradation of the whole world—for every person who would ever live!

It was absolutely overwhelming. No wonder the Saviour cried out, *My God, my God, why hast thou forsaken me?* (Matthew 27:46). God the Father had to turn His head because He could not look on sin (see Isaiah 59:2). So Jesus endured that anguish...alone. And because He took our sins, we can now come to God.

Jesus knows the awful sadness and bitterness sin produces. And because He took our sins upon himself, He can comfort us in any situation. The Word of God says, *For we have not an high priest which cannot be touched with the feeling of our infirmities; but was in all points tempted like as we are, yet without sin. Let us therefore come boldly unto the throne of grace, that we may obtain mercy, and find grace to help in time of need* (Hebrews 4:15,16).

Were you there at the place of punishment from whence comes redemption?

The penalty for sin is death! That punishment must be endured—that penalty must be paid. And that was the reason for Christ's death on the cross—the purpose of Calvary. On that day, the place of punishment became the place of redemption for all mankind...for the whole world.

Without the gallows of Golgotha there could be no salvation, no forgiveness for sin, no redemption.

The old spiritual concludes by asking, "Were you there when He rose up from the grave?" Thank God, through Christ our Lord, we were there!

Through His sacrifice, we've faced death and overcome it with life everlasting.

We've gone through the darkness of this world and moved into His marvelous light.

We've overcome the desperation of unquenchable thirst by receiving a well of living water springing up within our souls.

We've found the only source of joy and blessings that overcomes life's sorrows, and the only comfort in the time of anguish and tears.

And we've met Jesus at the place of punishment and found it has become a place of redemption.

Only by going to Calvary to see what Christ has done for us can we really experience the full joy of Easter! Were YOU there?

Oh, truly, "sometimes it causes me to tremble" to realize how much we owe...how rich we are. My mind can scarcely comprehend the wonder of it all. How marvelous!

No wonder Jesus commissioned us to go tell this great good news to every person in all the world! Let's go tell it to all who will hear!

9

Right Where I Am!

You and I are missionaries.

We really are—we have been called to share the gospel and help win lost and unsaved people to Christ on the mission fields of the earth.

I can almost hear someone saying, "Oh, Rexella, I could never be a missionary and do great things for the Lord in some far country. I don't have eloquent words or deep spiritual wisdom, and I'll probably never have the opportunity to go very far away from my own neighborhood. So there's really not very much I can do."

Do the little things

My response is simple—we can pay attention to little things. I have been so challenged by the admonition of Horatio Bonar, who said—"It is well to remember that a holy life is made up of a number of small things. Little words—not eloquent speeches or sermons. Little deeds—not miracles in battles. Deeds—not one great heroic act of martyrdom—make up most Christian lives."

Isn't that tremendous? God is looking for someone to do the little deeds and say the simple things about Jesus—to live the everyday life of faith in their neighborhood. Don't belittle the opportunity He has given you. As the prophet said, *For who hath despised the day of small things?* (Zechariah 4:10).

Some years ago when Jack and I were conducting citywide crusades, I began to feel a strange yearning inside my being—a sense of unrest, of being unfulfilled. I couldn't understand it. We were on the road up to nine months out of the year, ministering to thousands of people every night. I was part of the team—I stood and sang to great crowds and sensed the presence of the Holy Spirit using my songs to speak to many precious souls. Along with this, I had the extreme pleasure each crusade of speaking to ladies' luncheons and various organizations. I found extreme joy in seeing many coming to the Lord during those afternoons.

Yet my inner spirit was not at peace. I felt a hunger to have a one-to-one experience of witnessing, to personally lead people to the Lord. As I prayed and sought God's guidance, the Lord seemed to say to me, "Yes, Rexella, there is a mission field for you outside the crusades. That mission field is right where you are—in the grocery store, at the shopping center, the coffee shop, or wherever you find yourself. The people you meet in these places need to know Me."

The Holy Spirit impressed on me that I needed to be aware of His leading and be ready to witness in the way He led me. For me, witnessing is not having a handful of gospel tracts to pass out on the sidewalk or asking a stranger passing by if I can explain the five spiritual laws and lead him to the Lord. Don't misunderstand me—I believe in using tracts and in being bold in sharing my testimony at times. But I've found that just showing love and being interested in people— getting to know them—prepares the way and makes more effective witnessing opportunities. How can I hope to lead a person to the Lord until I show enough genuine interest in her (or him) to get to know her?

A sales girl in a store I sometimes visit said to me one day, "Mrs. Van Impe, you're the only one who ever really looks at *me*."

Sow good seeds

It's important to use the tools of kindness and simple friendship to break the ground and till the soil. Then you plant a seed or two, and water them faithfully with the Word of God. The day will come when those seeds will grow and be ready to harvest. You may have the opportunity of reaping—or someone else may be there at just the right moment to lead that person to Christ. As the great Apostle Paul wrote, *I have planted, Apollos watered; but God gave the increase* (1 Corinthians 3:6).

One of the sweetest compliments I've ever received came from a dear lady who is not of our faith. I have tried to let my life witness to her for several years as she has waited on me at one of my favorite stores.

As I stood talking with her one day, another customer came up, purchased something, and asked, "May I have one of those special shopping bags?"

"I'm so sorry," said my friend. "You have to make a purchase of at least $15 to get the decorative bag."

I said to the lady, "Oh, please take my shopping bag. You seem to like it and I have others at home."

The lady behind the counter smiled at the customer and said, "Let me introduce you to Mrs. Van Impe, she's a real Christian." I found that her words warmed my heart and blessed my soul.

I've found that when I show love and quietly minister in little ways to the people who cross my path, the Lord satisfies the yearning of my heart to be used to win someone to Him.

Although I've tried to be a good witness to everyone I possibly could, it had been a long while since I'd personally prayed with an individual to accept the Lord. There is no greater thrill than this!

I am humbly grateful for the opportunity Jack and I have to be on international TV and to share the gospel to a great viewing audience each week. We receive thousands of letters each week, many from people who say they accepted the Lord as they watched our program.

Lead souls to Jesus

But there's nothing like leading someone to Jesus on a one-to-one basis. And that happened during an Open House event at our headquarters. A dear lady came up to me and introduced me to her grandson, who was about 21 years of age.

"I'd like for my grandson to be baptized," she said.

I looked at the young man and asked, "Why do you want to be baptized?"

"Oh," he said, obviously wishing to please his grandmother, "I think it would be a nice thing to do."

I said, "Well, according to the Bible, before you're baptized there are some things that have to happen. Have you been born again?"

"No," he replied.

"Do you know what that means?"

"No, I don't."

"Would you like to know?"

"Yes," he said, "I really would."

So the young man and I, along with a couple of other believers, went into my office and knelt down beside a chair. I explained the simple plan of salvation to him—how Jesus died to provide forgiveness of all sin. Then I asked if he needed the Lord.

"Oh, yes," he said, "I have done so many things wrong. I really want to accept Jesus as my Saviour."

So we prayed the sinner's prayer together, and that young man became a Christian. I don't know who was the happiest—him or me or his grandmother! It was wonderful.

Be a witness in your "world"

This can happen to you, too. You have a mission field to work for the Lord...right where you are. The Bible says, *The steps of a good man* [or woman] *are ordered by the Lord: and he delighteth in his way* (Psalm 37:23). Think of it—you don't take a single step by accident. God sends you wherever you go for a reason. Someone in your "world" needs to see the witness of your life and to hear your testimony in your everyday conversation. Don't ever forget this. The Bible says, *Moreover it is required in stewards, that a man* [or woman] *be found faithful* (1 Corinthians 4:2).

I read recently about a famous preacher who concluded a powerful sermon in a revival meeting and gave an invitation. A woman of great wealth and social distinction came down the aisle and asked if she could say a few words.

"I want you to know why I came forward tonight. It is not because of any word spoken by this good preacher. I stand here because of the influence of a little woman who sits before me. Her fingers are rough with toil, the hard work of many years has stooped her low.

She's just a poor, obscure washer woman who has served in my home for many years. I have never known her to be impatient, speak an unkind word, or do a dishonorable deed. But I know countless little acts of unselfish love that adorn her life.

"Shamefully, let me say that I have openly sneered in her face and laughed at her fidelity to God. Yet, when my little girl was taken away recently, it was this woman who caused me to look beyond the grave and shed my first tear of hope. The sweet magnetism of her life has led me to Christ. I covet the things that have made her life so beautiful."

When the woman finished speaking, the great preacher got up and said, "My friends, let me introduce you to the real preacher of the evening," and he had the little washer woman stand.

How effective a missionary this humble laundress was! Her life was a powerful witness right where she worked. She found her mission field without ever leaving home.

You and I can do the same thing if we will pay attention to little things...and live for Christ where we are. Remember, before the Lord told His disciples to go *unto the uttermost part of the earth,* He asked them to be witnesses unto Him *in Jerusalem, and in all Judaea, and in Samaria* (Acts 1:8).

He has not changed His plan or His commission! He has called you to be His witness, starting in your own neighborhood, to the people of your own town, to your own "world."

Say not ye, There are yet four months, and then cometh harvest? behold, I say unto you, Lift up your eyes, and look on the fields; for they are white already to harvest (John 4:35).

Pray ye therefore the Lord of the harvest, that he will send forth labourers into his harvest (Matthew 9:38).

When you pray this prayer, be ready to have it answered by God tapping YOU on the shoulder! Isaiah told of hearing the voice of God, saying, *Whom shall I send, and who will go for us? Then said I, Here am I; send me. And he said, Go, and tell this people* (Isaiah 6:8,9).

Can you hear the voice of God today? Listen with the ears of your heart. Then take my hand, and let's get going to our mission field...right where we are!

10

"Just a Cup of Coffee, Please!"

The news media often calls attention to the large number of homeless and hungry people in our nation's big cities. The scenes of people sleeping on benches, huddling in cardboard boxes, or looking through garbage cans for food are pitiful and troubling. While many of these individuals have ended up on the street through misfortunes beyond their control, even sadder are the cases who are there largely by choice.

As I prayed and thought about this problem, it occurred to me that while not homeless and destitute, most of us, in a spiritual sense, have gotten by with just a cup of coffee and a morsel of bread when we could have been feasting on God's plentiful banquet of spiritual manna. As the Apostle James observes, *Ye have not, because ye ask not* (James 4:2).

My husband, Jack, and I have a favorite little "home cookin'" cafe we often visit when it's just the two of us. It's not fancy at all, but it's a cozy, comfortable place where we can relax—and the food is good. We go there often enough that we know most of the waitresses and many of the regular customers.

For weeks we noticed that a certain man was almost always in the cafe, sitting at the counter. He looked as if he might be homeless, usually dressed in worn, slightly shabby clothes which probably hadn't been laundered in weeks. He was always alone—never did we see him with a friend or ever having a conversation with others at the counter. His countenance was drawn and sad, and one could sense that he had known much sorrow in his lifetime. The waitresses told us he ate only once a day—the rest of the time he just drank coffee..."buy one cup and the refills are free."

Jack and I felt terribly sorry for this man. One night as we were having a light dinner, we looked over at him sitting alone at the counter, nursing his coffee cup, and it made us sad. My hubby called a waitress over and said, "Give that man the best dinner in the house and bring me the bill. Let him pick out anything on the menu and tell him a friend has picked up the tab."

"No, Dr. Van Impe, you don't need to do that," said the waitress.

"But I want to," he answered. "He looks like he needs a good meal, and I'd just like to help him a little."

"You don't understand," she said. "That is Mr. _____" (and she named a very well-known and wealthy local family). "His father owned much of the land that is now the City of Troy—he's the heir to millions!"

"But he looks so underprivileged!" I exclaimed.

"Yes, I know," said the waitress, "but he's really a multimillionaire. He lives like a pauper by choice."

I haven't seen that poor, sad man lately, but recently I've been thinking about his situation. Could it be that many Christians are living like spiritual paupers when they could be enjoying God's manifest blessings every day of their lives? Are they settling for just a cup of coffee when they could be feasting at the Lord's banquet table?

As we face the future, are we anxious about what lies ahead? Will it be a time of happiness and blessing...or endless loneliness and deprivation?

Change your wardrobe

The old man in the cafe was dressed in worn, shabby clothes. Yet he could have been wearing the finest suit from the best tailor in town.

What are you wearing? The Prophet Isaiah said, *I will greatly rejoice in the Lord, my soul shall be joyful in my God; for he hath clothed me with the garments of salvation, he hath covered me with the robe of righteousness, as a bridegroom decketh himself with ornaments, and as a bride adorneth herself with her jewels* (Isaiah 61:10).

Clothe yourself in the wardrobe God has provided for you. Get dressed in His righteousness and see what a change His garments will make in your whole outlook on life. You'll discover a new awareness of God as your Sustainer and Protector. You'll stand taller and walk in trust and confidence.

So resolve to stop dressing like the world and get clothed in His righteousness.

Put sadness aside

The old man in the cafe looked so sad, as if the weight of the world was on his shoulders. Yes, from a worldly perspective, he had everything. He was from a prominent family, with every possible financial advantage at his disposal. If money could buy happiness, he could have had it all.

Christianity is the most joyful of all the world's religions. Yet we often manage to make it appear the most sad and mournful by our actions and our countenance. Mark Twain once had his famous character, Huck Finn, wondering if the mule in the barn had "got religion" because of its long face!

The psalmist exults, *Thou hast put gladness in my heart. For he satisfieth the longing soul, and filleth the hungry soul with goodness* (Psalm 4:7; 107:9).

I think we sometimes develop a bad habit of letting our faces reflect the care and confusion of the world around us instead of the joy and peace of the Lord welling up within us.

If we have full access to God's goodness, gladness, and blessedness, shouldn't our faces show it?

As Christians, our future is as bright as the promises of God. And the Word of God is filled with wonderful promises. Some of my favorites include Christ's promise: *Lo, I am with you alway, even unto the end of the world* (Matthew 28:20) and also God's assurance that *as thy days, so shall thy strength be* (Deuteronomy 33:25).

87

If we believe God, we have something to smile about.

Be a friend

In all the times we observed the old man in the cafe, Jack and I never saw him with a friend...or ever being friendly with those around him. While others had pleasant conversations and shared personal things with each other, the old man sat alone, without a friend. How sad.

But while true friendship is measured by more than "hellos" and conversations, some people have no friends because they will let no one get close to them.

As the writer of Proverbs observes, *A man that hath friends must show himself friendly: and there is a friend that sticketh closer than a brother* (Proverbs 18:24).

One must be a friend to others to have friends who will share fellowship and companionship in return. And this is an important part of life. But even if earthly friends do fail in times of trouble, we can be secure in knowing that we can have a friend who will stick closer than a brother, in good times and bad.

We know we can count on Him because He has said, *I will never leave thee, nor forsake thee* (Hebrews 13:5).

When we have such a Friend, why don't we rely on Him more? In the words of the grand old gospel song, "What a Friend We Have in Jesus,"

Oh, what peace we often forfeit,
    Oh, what needless pain we bear,
All because we do not carry
    Everything to God in prayer.

Eat heartily

I don't think I'll ever forget the old man in the cafe, scrimping by on one meal a day, when he could have had anything on the menu, anytime he wanted it. Yet he'd order "Just a cup of coffee, please" and ask for free refills. How tragic to see a multimillionaire going hungry.

But how much more tragic to have the riches of heaven at our disposal and go through life starving ourselves spiritually! Do you have a Bible? Of course, you do. Are you feasting daily on the abundant nourishment found there...or do you hurriedly pull out a single scripture card and glance at it before you dash out into the day?

Compare your biblical diet with Jeremiah's. He said, *Thy words were found, and I did eat them; and thy word was unto me the joy and rejoicing of mine heart: for I am called by thy name, O Lord God of hosts* (Jeremiah 15:16).

Don't settle for just a cup of coffee—eat heartily—even as the Apostle Peter admonished us to do in 1 Peter 2:2, stating: *As newborn babes, desire the sincere milk of the word, that ye may grow thereby.* The psalmist concurs, saying, *O taste and see that the Lord is good: blessed is the man that trusteth in him* (Psalm 34:8).

I heard the story of a man whose dream was to go to America. For years he saved his money to buy passage on a ship. Finally he had just enough, with only a small amount left over.

He took part of the little money he had left and bought some bread and cheese he could take on board. By careful rationing, he thought there would be just enough to last through the voyage.

So he set sail, glad to finally be going to the "promised land." Other passengers were festive and happy, going into the ship's dining room to eat wonderful meals, and strolling about the decks, laughing and having refreshments together.

The man would go to his little cabin at mealtime and eat stale bread and hard cheese.

But he had miscalculated the length of the voyage, and a few days before the ship was to arrive in New York harbor, he ran out of food. He drank water and did without for a day or so. Then he got so hungry he didn't think he could last. So he scraped together all the money he had left—several coins—and went to a steward in the dining room.

"Excuse me, please," he said. "Is this enough money to buy just a little bit to eat? I've run out of food and I'm very hungry."

The steward said, "Sir, you do not need to pay extra to eat in the dining room. Your meals were paid for in the price of your ticket."

I urge you to begin living up to your privileges in God. Jesus Christ paid for them in the price of your passage to heaven!

Blessing, gladness, satisfaction, goodness, and all other spiritual pleasures are yours. *Happy is he that hath the God of Jacob for his help, whose hope is in the Lord his God* (Psalm 146:5).

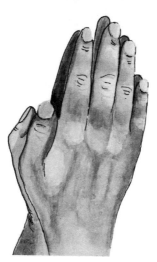

11

Is God Listening?

Some time ago I contracted a dangerous viral infection which threatened the sight of my left eye and produced severe discomfort and pain. Just as I was getting a little better, I came down with pneumonia in my right lung.

During this time of unusual stress and trauma, Jack and I spent even more time than normal praying and seeking God. Thank the Lord, He heard and answered our prayers!

Experiencing those wearisome days when I might have been tempted to ask, "Does God care? Is He listening?"—I found new assurance that *the Lord, the Creator of the ends of the earth, fainteth not, neither is weary* (Isaiah 40:28). And I can truthfully say with the psalmist that *I waited patiently for the Lord; and he inclined unto me, and heard my cry* (Psalm 40:1).

While prayer has always been an important part of our lives and ministry, now it has become even more vital—an integral part of the very fabric of Jack's life and mine. Prayer has become as natural as breathing to me, and has carried me into the Father's presence where I draw directly from His unlimited strength.

In the times of testing I often felt as if the Lord comforted me by saying, "Pray." And in saying "Come to me," He also said, "Wait patiently." It has been my experience that life's difficulties may sometimes be meant for the strengthening of one's heart and soul.

The power of prayer

When we enter into prayer, we enter into the realm of divine omnipotence and tap into the unlimited power of God. Prayer leaps over boundaries, stops at no distances, and balks at no obstacles. No wonder Jesus said, *With men it is impossible, but not with God: for with God all things are possible* (Mark 10:27).

The late Dr. M. R. DeHaan recognized the tremendous force God placed in the hands of His people through prayer. DeHaan said, "I would far rather have the power of prayer to move the powers of heaven, than to have the power of preaching to move the masses on earth."

While some of us may not have the gift of preaching or the anointed eloquence to proclaim the gospel to all who will hear—all of us do have the power of prayer at our disposal. We can commune directly with our Creator, and cry out to the God of the universe with the steadfast assurance that HE IS LISTENING... and He will answer.

Why, then, do we go about laden with burdens too heavy to bear? Why do we endure overwhelming sorrows and pain? Why do we attempt to make the best of living with want and lack? The Lord gently scolds us for failing to seek His help by saying, *Ye have not, because ye ask not* (James 4:2).

I love the grand old gospel song that asks, "Are you weary, are you heavy-hearted?" then responds, "Tell it to Jesus, Tell it to Jesus!" On and on the song goes, listing man's most common troubles and fears, and always reminding, urging, commanding—"Tell it to Jesus alone!"

God has invited us to come to Him with our needs and burdens. Jesus said, *Ask, and it shall be given you; seek, and ye shall find; knock, and it shall be opened unto you: for every one that asketh receiveth; and he that seeketh findeth; and to him that knocketh it shall be opened* (Matthew 7:7).

Are the answers you need being given? Have you asked?

Are you finding the solutions to life's problems? Are you seeking?

Are the doors of opportunity being opened to you? Are you knocking?

God is ready and willing to meet your every need. He is more than enough for all your problems. But to receive what He wants you to have, you have to take the first step. Have you ever taught your children to come to you for assistance with their needs? Even though you sometimes knew what they needed before they asked, have you ever waited until they made their petition to you?

Jesus said, *If ye then, being evil, know how to give good gifts unto your children, how much more shall your Father which is in heaven give good things to them that ask him?* (Matthew 7:11).

So we need to learn to ask—we need to be sure to make our petitions known to God through prayer.

Pray in faith

Then, too, we must pray with faith. Some people feel their faith is too weak, but I believe, with the Apostle Paul, that *God hath dealt to every man the measure of faith* (Romans 12:3). If our faith comes from God—if He has provided it for us, then we have enough...and it is sufficient!

When in the midst of suffering and in need of healing, many of us may find it difficult to receive healing directly from the hand of God. But the Lord often uses other hands, other instruments to meet our need. Often healing comes through the channel of doctors and medicine. Depending on such healing aids is not necessarily a lack of faith.

An old motto I've heard suggests that we should work as though everything depended on us, but pray as if everything depended on God. Perhaps this is the perfect blending of faith and works endorsed by the Apostle James (see 2:20-26).

I thank God for the fine doctors and "miracle" drugs employed in my treatment during my illness. But I am absolutely convinced that prayer helped speed my healing by making my body more receptive to the treatment than it ordinarily would have been.

I recovered with no lasting ill effects, no scars, no permanent damage. Yet, another lady with almost the same condition, being treated by the same doctor, with the same medication, did experience facial scarring and ongoing trauma.

Is God really interested in our individual needs and problems? Aren't our personal difficulties too small to bring to the attention of the Almighty? Isn't He preoccupied with wars and cataclysmic events, interested only in global and universal affairs?

Not at all! Nothing is too great or too small to bring to the Lord. He knows! He sees! He cares! Oh, yes, my friend, He is listening...and He will answer.

I know this—when our own strength and provision fail, prayer helps us tap into an inexhaustible divine supply. And it is undeniably true that more miracles are wrought by prayer than this world could ever imagine.

The Holy Spirit intercedes

Dr. Van Impe and I are finding that when we pray, the Holy Spirit directs us and helps us to pray. We do not have to depend on long prayer lists and "vain repetitions" that become meaningless rituals (see Matthew 6:7).

There are times when I feel so overwhelmed by needs or challenges before me that I don't even know how to pray. But the Holy Spirit does—and He ministers through me to touch the heart of God. Paul wrote, *Likewise the Spirit also helpeth our infirmities: for we know not what we should pray for as we ought: but the Spirit* [himself] *maketh intercession for us with groanings which cannot be uttered* (Romans 8:26).

There have been times when I knelt to pray and could only weep—I couldn't find the words to express what was inside. I would cry out, "Oh God, I don't know how to put this because I'm so burdened." What a comfort to know that the Holy Spirit went right on interceding for me with groanings and expressions too deep to be uttered.

And sooner or later, as I waited before God on my knees, that deep peace that passes all understanding would sweep over me, and my troubled spirit would be at rest. Once again I would have the blessed assurance of knowing that *all things work together for good to them that love God, to them who are the called according to his purpose* (Romans 8:28).

My friend, what God has done for me, He will do for you. The Lord is ready to minister to you in every part of your life. He is listening.

TAKE TIME TO PRAY

I got up quite early one morning
    And rushed right into the day;
I had so much to accomplish
    I took no time out to pray.

The problems just tumbled about me,
    And heavier came every task;
"Why doesn't God help me," I wondered,
    He said, "Why, you didn't ask!"

I saw naught of joy or of beauty—
    The day sped on, gray and bleak;
I asked, "Why won't the Lord show me?"
    He said, "But you didn't seek!"

I tried to come into God's presence;
    I used all my keys at the lock,
God gently, lovingly chided,
    "My child, why didn't you knock?"

I woke up quite early this morning
    And paused ere entering the day;
There was so much to accomplish
    I HAD TO TAKE TIME TO PRAY!

12
Let Me Cry!

I've been doing some crying, lately.

Many times in the past several months, I've wept over the suffering and physical deterioration of my beloved father-in-law, Oscar Van Impe. Seeing this dedicated, once-strong man of God (who prayed five hours a day for the needs of others) lying weak and helpless really tears my heart out. Repeated strokes and heart attacks confine him to bed...and he can barely speak. When I see him—often when I simply think of his condition—I cry.

My own precious mother, who is perhaps one of the few saints I know on earth, also has been stricken with a very serious problem, accompanied with excruciating pain. Mother has been graced with many gifts from God—among them the gifts of help and encouragement. The morning I took her to the hospital for diagnostic x-rays, she asked two favors of me. "Please turn in my donation check for the ministry, and would you mind taking me by the post office so I can mail some get-well cards?"

She has been the most unselfish, thoughtful, and Christlike person one could ever meet in this world. Our family of employees tells me that when she is in the office, she exudes the fruits of the Spirit to such a degree that the very atmosphere is charged by her joy and love.

Doctors discovered that Mother has a non-cancerous brain tumor and an inflamed major artery in the brain. They feel that at her age, surgery or other aggressive treatment is not the best treatment for her, so they are trying to control the pain and make her comfortable.

Seeing her pain makes me cry. What a comfort it has been to have a precious husband and dear friends who have wept with me during this trial.

A while back I noticed that a young waitress who often serves Jack and me when we go out to eat seemed unusually quiet and withdrawn and there was a strain on her countenance. When I went to wash my hands in the ladies room, I had a chance to pull her aside and ask if something was wrong. Tears spilled down her cheeks as she told me her husband had just asked her for a divorce.

Imagine the pain of having your husband or wife look you in the eye and say, "I don't love you anymore—I want out of this marriage." I can't even begin to comprehend the shock, sorrow, and grief one would feel in such a situation.

I didn't know what to say to this poor girl —but I put my arms around her and comforted her the only way I knew how...with my tears.

Also in recent months, I have felt an increased burden for my unsaved friends and loved ones. Bible prophecy makes it so clear that time on this old earth is running out fast and that surely Jesus is coming soon...perhaps today! So I have been praying...and weeping ...for my unsaved loved ones. It is the only way I know to minister to them!

What is a tear?

The great preacher, T. DeWitt Talmage, once wrote, "Help me explain a tear. A chemist will tell you that it is made up of salt and lime and other component parts; but he misses the chief ingredients—the acid of a soured life, the viperine sting of a bitter memory, the fragments of a broken heart. I will tell you what a tear is: it is agony in solution."

These are powerful, moving words. And perhaps all of us have either witnessed or personally experienced the truth Talmage sought to convey.

But I suggest to you that there is more to tears than sadness, sorrow, regret, and pain. Tears can be a release from stress and anxiety, a vent for frustration, a safety valve for overpowering emotions. Tears can be the most sincere expression of compassion and love. And just as raindrops wash the smoke, smog, and impurities from the atmosphere, so tears can wash away the stains of bitterness and disappointment from our souls.

A time to weep

As Solomon, perhaps the wisest man who ever lived, once declared, *To every thing there is a season, and a time to every purpose under the heaven...A time to weep, and a time to laugh* (Ecclesiastes 3:1,4).

We live in a time when everyone wants to laugh all the time, but no one is willing to weep. And if someone does cry, it makes people really uncomfortable. Children are hushed and told not to cry. Men are taught that tears don't go with a macho image...that only sissies cry. And women who weep at some sadness or loss are interrupted and advised to wipe their eyes and get control of themselves.

No! No! No! Let me cry. It's all right to cry. I need to cry. In fact, one of my goals is to minister to those who are weeping. I want to do all I can, to say what I can...and when there are no deeds or words that can help, to weep with them.

Perhaps my resolution is best expressed in the words of the late Bob Pierce in his moving book, *Let My Heart Be Broken With the Things That Break the Heart of God.*

When Jesus wept, His tears were for others. Both Matthew and Luke describe how He wept over the city of Jerusalem for those who would not hear and accept the Truth! We, too, should weep for others.

Weep over souls

Should we be less concerned over lost souls than our Saviour? Why are we not crying and praying for the lost to be saved before it is eternally too late?

I've seen people moved to tears by the plight of fictional characters in a paperback book. A melodramatic film may jokingly be described as a "two-hanky" movie, and it's perfectly all right. But the same people who get involved and empathize with artificial stories can see real live people around them dying and slipping into eternity without God and never feel a twinge or shed a tear.

I wonder—if the unsaved friends and loved ones I'm praying for don't seem to be any closer to the Lord than when I first started, could it be because I haven't shed any tears for them? The Bible says, *They that sow in tears shall reap in joy. He that goeth forth and weepeth, bearing precious seed, shall doubtless come again with rejoicing, bringing his sheaves with him* (Psalm 126:5,6).

Weep over sin

Sometimes I can hardly watch the news on television or read the daily paper without crying. My heart breaks at what is going on in our nation and the world today. There is such evil and perversion, such wickedness and violence. How long will God allow men's hearts to be filled with such deliberate, willful sin before calling them to judgment?

I believe we are to weep over sin, whether our own, our family's, or our nation's. The Apostle Paul wrote, *For godly sorrow worketh repentance to salvation* (2 Corinthians 7:10).

I am reminded of how Peter, after denying the Lord during the awful hours before the Crucifixion, *went out, and wept bitterly*

(Matthew 26:75). Those tears of repentance led to his being forgiven and restored.

Weep over sorrow

Just as there is a time to weep over souls and a time to weep over sin, there is also a time to weep over sorrow. Do you remember when Mary and Martha showed the Lord the tomb where their brother Lazarus was buried? The Bible says, *Jesus wept* (John 11:35).

There is a time for sorrow...and when it comes, tears are appropriate. Paul instructed, *Rejoice with them that do rejoice, and weep with them that weep* (Romans 12:15).

Notice that the verse did not say to laugh with those who are laughing and to tell those who are crying to stop and cheer up. No, it says to cry with those who are crying! That means to share their sorrow—to get down under the burden with them. And when you share their tears—when all you can do is cry with them—you'll find it is a tremendously effective way to minister your compassion and love.

I once interviewed a pastor who had suffered the traumatic loss of his little son. This man told me that in the midst of his grieving, the people of his church did not understand or know how to weep with him. They would come to him and say, "Pastor, why are you crying? Don't you have any faith?"

After a while this minister wrote a book about what he had learned during his sorrowful experience. He called it, *Jonathan, You Left Too Soon*. But the main lesson I learned from his experience was that in the day of sorrow, it's okay to weep. In fact, for most people, it's a really good way to cope with loss and grief and begin to heal the broken heart and crushed emotions. Tears can be tremendously therapeutic.

I know I have been made acutely aware of the value of tears. And I pray that God will make me willing to weep with those who weep, whether they cry tears of pain, heartache, sorrow...or joy! I encourage you to consider whether God can also use you in a ministry of tears.

Remember, though, that our tears will not —cannot—last long. The psalmist sang, *Weeping may endure for a night, but joy cometh in the morning* (Psalm 30:5).

I'm here to tell you that a great morning is coming soon, when we will all be in the presence of the Lord. Oh, what a glorious promise and steadfast hope! For on that glad day, *God shall wipe away all tears from their eyes; and there shall be no more death, neither sorrow, nor crying, neither shall there be any more pain: for the former things are passed away* (Revelation 21:4).

No wonder Jesus said, *Blessed are ye that weep now: for ye shall laugh* (Luke 6:21).

13

The Purr-fect Blessing

For more than seventeen years, our cat, Fenica, was a great source of companionship and enjoyment to Jack and me. But after all those years, she finally succumbed to a fatal disease after suffering for several months. She was an important part of our lives. In earlier years, she was bright and friendly and had the uncanny ability to endear herself to folks rather quickly.

A few years ago I wrote about how I found this abandoned, sick, starving creature and persuaded Jack to let me feed and nurse her back to health.

At first Dr. Van Impe would only consent for Fenica to stay out on the patio...then we let her into the garage on cold nights. From there she moved straight into our hearts—and she was an important member of our family from that day on.

Over the years, quite a "love affair" developed between Jack and this soft, furry creature. Most people envision my husband as a very serious, scholarly man who thinks of nothing but Bible study and prayer. And he does spend many hours daily with his Bible and study material.

But I wish you could have seen him and Fenica on the floor, rolling around and playing their own games. They had a great relationship—and some pretty silly conversations! I really don't know what all they talked about together, but from Fenica's expressions and faithful attentiveness, it seemed obvious that she understood and appreciated every word Jack said.

A praying cat?

Of course, it was love at first sight for this little cat and me. And over the years she was so much company and a real friend. Often Fenica joined me as I knelt to pray. As I poured my heart out to God, I'd feel my little kitty snuggling up beside me.

During the dark days a few years back when the ministry was struggling with great financial difficulties and the stress seemed almost overwhelming, I was able to survive only by laying my burdens at the feet of the Lord. In those prayer times, when words failed me and tears coursed down my cheeks, how comforting it was to hear a gentle purr and to be suddenly—thrillingly—aware that I was not alone...that God's presence was all around me!

Jack and I started out to help and care for a neglected and needy animal. But in exchange for some medical attention and a little food, Fenica became a great source of joy and blessing to us. Only now—after she is gone—are we beginning to understand why the Lord sent this little creature into our lives.

Pets are good for your health

Scientists have begun to find proof of what they only suspected before—that contact with animals has specific effects on the human body and mind. Health officials have verified that pets have definite therapeutic value in people's regular daily lives, and also for people in institutions. Hospitals, nursing homes, and penal institutions have discovered the positive impact animals can have on handicapped or socially maladjusted individuals. Some of them regularly bring animals into therapy sessions for patients and inmates, and puppies and kittens often get responses from people no one else had been able to reach.

As early as 1790, a Quaker group in England discovered the value of taking mentally handicapped people on group retreats and encouraging them to roam the grounds and spend time with farm animals. This therapy seemed to get tremendous results compared with the limited institutional treatment available at that time.

Organizations like the Latham Foundation of Alameda, California, and the Delta Society of Renton, Washington, promote interest in human-animal bonding and study the role animals play in human development.

Studies have shown that encouraging abused children to be responsible for caring for animals—especially disabled or injured creatures—provides a real psychological boost. Perhaps just seeing how another helpless, hurting creature can overcome the odds and survive gives them hope.

But the benefit of association with animals is not just psychological. Studies show that the heart rate is lower when people are in the presence of a friendly animal. And elderly people with pets make fewer visits to the doctor. Perhaps we are discovering a new form of low cost preventive health care.

Of course, it's really not new at all. I believe it is highly significant that in the beginning, God *first* gave Adam the animals and birds to keep him from being lonely. Genesis 2:18,19 says, *And the Lord God said, It is not good that the man should be alone; I will make him an help meet for him. And out of the ground the Lord God formed every beast of the field, and every fowl of the air; and brought them unto Adam to see what he would call them.*

I believe that in most cases, animals want to be the friends of man, not enemies. Most animals become hostile or vicious only out of fear or as a result of being abused by man.

Animals have great value

How important are animals to us? We've already seen that God provided them to Adam even before He gave him Eve. That's pretty important! And later on, when the wickedness of man became intolerable to God in Noah's day, not only did the Lord devise a plan to save representatives of the family of man from the destruction of the flood, He also arranged to save at least one pair of every species of animal!

God regards His creatures as beautiful and valuable. And so should we. There are many ways they can be of service to us...and there is much we can learn from them.

Wisdom from a pet

I remember a cold winter's day when I walked into our bedroom to look for a book I'd left there. It was freezing cold outside, with snow on the ground, but the rays of the sun were streaming through the window.

Fenica was stretched out in a chair by the window, soaking up the warmth of the sun. When she heard me come in, she stretched her head back and looked at me upside down...but didn't move. It was almost as if she were saying, "I don't have a worry in the world—I have you to keep me safe and warm."

I found my book and went back downstairs, but I found myself thinking how wonderful it would be if I could learn to trust and rest in the Lord's love the way our cat confidently and comfortably depended on Jack and me.

As Jesus said in His Sermon on the Mount, *If ye then, being evil, know how to give good gifts unto your children* [or pets], *how much more shall your Father which is in heaven give good things to them that ask him?* (Matthew 7:11).

116

So perhaps we all could take some lessons in living from precious pets like Fenica.

- She trusted me and knew I loved her and would not hurt her or allow her to be injured—and I can trust God (see John 3:16; 1 John 3:16; Galatians 2:20; Ephesians 2:4,5).
- My cat relied on me to direct her and not let danger fall in her path—and I can rely on God (see Proverbs 3:5,6).
- Fenica knew I cared for her and that I would take care of her, so she was not burdened down with concern. I can cast my care on the Lord, for He cares for me (see 1 Peter 5:7).
- No matter what she needed, Fenica turned to me as her source of supply. And I can have that same relationship with my heavenly Father, who supplies *all* [my] *need according to his riches in glory by Christ Jesus* (Philippians 4:19).

And finally, Fenica loved to be with Jack and me. Wherever we were in the house, she tried to be near us. Often, even when I walked through the house, she would go along with me. She didn't need anything—she wasn't asking for anything...she just wanted to be near me and have fellowship with me. And that was so very special to me.

How much more must our heavenly Father enjoy having us want to spend time in His presence and have fellowship with Him? There's a wonderful inspirational song that says, "I'll walk with God." It speaks of having God beside us to lead and guide us.

What a thrill to be able to have personal fellowship with our Creator, who is also our Friend. Nothing in life can ever defeat us when we walk with Him.

It really is...*The Perfect Blessing*.

14

I Remember Mother

I can't even begin to imagine how Mary must have felt on the day the angel told her the Holy Spirit would come upon her and that she would become the mother of the Messiah.

No doubt many Jewish girls dreamed of being chosen for such an honor, but they had no idea of what price would have to be paid by the maiden who became the mother of Jesus. How many virgins would have had the faith and steadfastness in God to receive this unique ministration of the Holy Spirit? And how many would have had the strength of character to endure the shame of being found with child before her marriage?

What a remarkable person Mary must have been. No doubt she was the ultimate of womanhood or God would not have chosen her to bear His Son. And surely her unswerving faith and devotion to duty are unexcelled in the pages of human history.

What a profound inspiration and influence her life of humble trust in God must have been for the boy Jesus as He *increased in wisdom and stature* (Luke 2:52) during His growing-up years in Nazareth. The Lord must have come to know His mother in a very special way during the nearly 30 years He lived with her and Joseph.

At the end of His life and ministry, Jesus must have remembered many things about His mother. No doubt He recalled her loving concern and patience when she traveled back to Jerusalem to find Him, at age twelve, still in the Temple with the elders.

And He must have remembered her trusting faith and her recognition of His divine nature at the wedding in Cana. Although He did not promise to remedy the shortage of wine (fruit of the vine), Mary confidently told the servants, *Whatsoever he saith unto you, do it* (John 2:5).

Jesus knew Mary's gracious spirit all of His life. With His divine nature, He could also see her heart, for He knew all of mankind. And yet Mary continued, with dignity, to be His mother. What a pure life she must have had.

Jesus remembered and respected His mother. On the cross just before He died, He looked down and saw her there, when so many others had forsaken Him. And in the hour of His greatest agony, carrying the awful burden of the sins of the world, He remembered Mary and made provision for her care. Seeing the Apostle John near her, He said, *Woman, behold thy son!* And to John, *Behold thy mother!* (John 19:26,27).

Precious memories

I remember my mother with every bit of admiration and respect that I think Jesus had for His mother. So much of *who* I am and *what* I am is a result of her loving guidance and positive influence. I first learned love at Mother's knee through her touch, her care. Then she pointed me to the love of Christ, and I was reared in a Christian home.

It was from Mother's voice that I first heard music, which has been such an important part of my whole life and ministry. In one of my earliest childhood memories, I am in her arms and she is singing! I have no doubt that my love for music came from her—I started singing when I was 5 years old.

I learned the discipline of my life from Mother. She never allowed me to sing in public unless I had my song memorized. I did not play the piano for others unless I had practiced.

Humility was a quality Mother taught me by example. To this day she has the most beautiful, unassuming spirit of anyone I know. To me she is a perfectly blended combination of the biblical sisters, Mary and Martha. She always spent time worshiping the Lord—I've walked into her bedroom many times and found her on her knees or reading her Bible. But her personal devotions were always balanced with service to others.

My Mother was—and is—a servant of the Lord and people. She goes out of her way to help, and nothing is ever too much for her to do. I've watched her bake for her friends, do laundry for a sick person, or make phone calls to encourage others when she was weary herself. She always would take time to send cards for funerals, birthdays, or other occasions when a friendly note would be appreciated.

I remember Mother taking me to church revivals where I had been invited to sing.

When we walked inside together, she would say to me, "Go ahead, honey, serve the Lord." And she would stay near the back of the church, not wanting to be noticed.

To this day, at age 83, Mother stays busy serving the Lord. The staff at our Jack Van Impe Ministries office love to have her come around. "Things are just better when she's around," they say. "She lightens the day and brings an extra measure of love and harmony."

Inner beauty

From Mother, I learned the secret of inner beauty—of filling my heart and mind with love and wholesomeness and letting them permeate my entire being. And I also learned the importance of always trying to look my best and having my home clean and in order.

Mother always kept herself beautifully groomed and modestly dressed, and her home immaculate. She taught me that appearance is important because it reflects the kind of person one truly is inside...and is a testimony— good or bad—for the Lord.

There are so many other qualities my mother taught me—tenderness, a sense of duty, a living expression of the gifts of the Holy Spirit. Space doesn't permit a listing of even half the good things she imparted to me by instruction and example.

But I must mention one more—I learned wisdom through my mother. Wisdom comes from the Lord, according to the Book of Proverbs. But Mother certainly was a living symbol of that divinely-given quality. She almost always had the answers to my questions, always knew the right thing to do in every situation, always seemed to know when to act and when to wait.

And although she didn't have the opportunity to complete school when she was young, later in life she went back to school and took some business courses. She did it on her own, just because she wanted a little better formal education—and because there were still some things she wanted to know about!

Like Ruth and Naomi

Not only was I blessed with a wonderful mother, but my mother-in-law and I had a beautiful relationship as well. I appreciated her so much. We never had the conflicts that many women seem to experience. We had more of a Ruth and Naomi relationship.

My mother-in-law has a very keen sense of humor and a love of life, which my husband shares. And she also displays a sweet sense of trust and faith.

My husband's parents returned to Belgium, their homeland, as missionaries, when their only child, Jack, was 17. He had just entered Bible school to prepare himself for the ministry. There were no other Van Impe relatives in America, and my in-laws had no money to leave with their young son.

It must have taken a tremendous amount of faith for Mother Van Impe to leave her only child and go so far away. She had to commit him into the hands of God and trust that he would be all right.

I've also respected the fact that my mother-in-law was never concerned about earthly possessions. As missionaries, their income was very limited, requiring many sacrifices, but she was content. No one ever heard her complain, or express a desire for a better house or home furnishings, or clothing. Her priorities were straight—she was working for eternal rewards. She has always been precious to me personally.

A legacy of love

What a tremendous legacy both Dr. Van Impe and I have received from our mothers.

Each Christmas season when we celebrate the birth of our Lord Jesus Christ, I especially remember Mother. Let us all remember our mothers, how they have helped the living Christ to be born in our hearts.

We can never forget what she has meant to us. Every day in some way her positive influence lives on in our lives. As the Prophet Isaiah wrote, *And thine ears shall hear a word behind thee, saying, This is the way, walk ye in it, when ye turn to the right hand, and when ye turn to the left* (Isaiah 30:21).

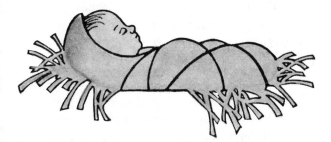

15

Is There Room in Your Heart for Him?

What a special time of the year! Thanksgiving and Christmas are more precious to me than any other holidays, and they so beautifully go hand in hand.

More and more, I realize the importance of being grateful for the true essence of Christmas—that God became flesh. He came as a baby, humbling himself to a manger and, one day, to Calvary's tree for you and me. Oh, what love!

I wonder if we can really understand the emotion in heaven and the joy on earth as

Mary and Joseph made their way to Bethlehem just prior to the birth of Christ.

An historic journey

Can you see them as they wearily make their way through the narrow streets of Bethlehem? Mary, tired from the long journey, sits on the little donkey as Joseph leads it along.

Their journey is almost over, and none too soon. They stop in front of one of the inns in Bethlehem. With a tender word, Joseph comforts his wife and then strides quickly toward the inn door.

Have you ever wondered what Mary was thinking as Joseph knocked at the innkeeper's door? Perhaps she was remembering what her cousin Elizabeth had said to her some time before. *Blessed art thou among women, and blessed is the fruit of thy womb. And whence is this to me, that the mother of my Lord should come to me? For, lo, as soon as the voice of thy salutation sounded in mine ears, the babe leaped in my womb for joy.*

And blessed is she that believed: for there shall be a performance [fulfillment] *of those things which were told her from the Lord* (Luke 1:42-45).

Mary knew how blessed she was for, out of all the women in the world, God had chosen her to give the world this baby. This wasn't Joseph's baby; He was the Son of God, produced by the Holy Spirit, waiting to be born in Bethlehem (see Luke 1:35 and Hebrews 10:5).

Mary knew about the promise that foretold: *But thou, Bethlehem Ephratah, though thou be little among the thousands of Judah, yet out of thee shall he come forth unto me that is to be ruler in Israel; whose goings forth have been from of old, from everlasting* (Micah 5:2).

Mary's mind didn't dare leap ahead to contemplate the rest of those words. It was enough for her to know that she was, at this very moment, in Bethlehem (ancestral home of King David, Joseph's forefather) and that her time to give birth was at hand.

Mary looked at Joseph, footsore and fatigued from walking alongside the donkey all the way so that she could ride. She knew how blessed she was to have this good and just man as her husband. He had handled the situation so well. He had shown her nothing but love and concern. More than once he had told her, "I know, beloved wife, that this child has been conceived in a special way. The angel laid all my fears to rest."

Joseph had learned of Mary's pregnancy after she returned from visiting Elizabeth. For six months they had marveled at the conversations they had each had with the angel. It must have been awesome for them, realizing that the Holy Ghost had visited Mary and that the child she carried was a divine original.

"Oh, Joseph," I can hear Mary saying, "He is to be called 'the Son of God.'"

"Yes, Mary," Joseph responded, "and His name is to be called JESUS, for He shall save His people from their sins."

The prophecy

Did they recall the words of Isaiah? Did they repeat those names? *Behold, a virgin shall conceive, and bear a son, and shall call his name Immanuel...For unto us a child is born, unto us a son is given: and the government shall be upon his shoulder: and his name shall be called Wonderful, Counsellor, The mighty God, The everlasting Father, The Prince of Peace* (Isaiah 7:14; 9:6).

Perhaps Mary remembered those conversations as her husband knocked at the inn-keeper's door. She was so tired. The journey had been long and hard. But now, at last, they had arrived in Bethlehem.

For us, today, a journey to Bethlehem is still not easy. In the hustle and bustle of the season, there are many things to deter us. We've all heard that we should keep Christ in Christmas, but let's be sure that we keep *our-*

selves in Christmas, as well! If we are not careful, we can become so busy with Yuletide activities that we are exhausted before we get to Bethlehem—and miss the real Christmas altogether.

Knock...knock...knock! Joseph knocks at the innkeeper's door. A *Baby* is about to be born—the most important Baby ever to be born on this earth. "Let us in...let Him in...out of the cold and darkness of the night." But the Bible tells us *there was no room for them in the inn* (Luke 2:7).

No room! Those are heart-rending words. Would we have said that? Yet, isn't it being said every day? We are all innkeepers, with room for many things, but do we have room for Him? In our lives—shabby stables that they are—He may be cradled, but *we* must give Him room.

Joseph, the rugged carpenter of Nazareth, a *just* man whose faith transcended his misgivings, enfolded Mary's helplessness in his strong arms as he lifted her off the back of the little donkey. Someone had tapped him on his sagging shoulders and said, "There is a place, if your wife won't mind. I know I can fix it and make it clean. It will be quiet there...and warm."

Lowly beginnings

Joseph had ministered to Mary's needs in that weary pilgrimage to Bethlehem; but his husbandly duties had not yet ended. *Mary in a stable? The Son of God born in a barn?* How his mind must have reeled. Remember, he was very human.

Husband, would you like for your wife to give birth to her firstborn in a stable? What lowly circumstances! *The Lord of all heaven and earth was about to make His human presence known in the world—but in a barn?* This was not the birthplace Joseph had imagined for JESUS.

Barns smell, not just of clean hay, but of animals. Barns are not always sanitary. Oh, the lovely Nativity scenes that we see at Christmas do not begin to portray what Joseph and Mary must have experienced in those pre-birth moments, as they contemplated their plight.

One wishes we could push back the pages of time and make it different—different, perhaps, like the school Christmas play I heard about.

One little boy had been asked to play the role of the innkeeper in the play. His parents, schoolmates, and teachers were so excited and pleased for him because he wasn't quite "normal" like the other boys and girls. Still, they wanted to include him in the performance.

Seven little words

His were simple lines. When Joseph knocked at the door and asked for a room, he, the innkeeper, would say, "There is no room in the inn." Seven words. And that was all.

The big night came. Practice perfomances had gone well. Then came that moment.

Knock...knock...knock—Joseph knocks at the inn door. With great emotion and convincing reality, Joseph presents his case to the innkeeper. His wife is *very* pregnant. In fact, the baby is due any moment. Won't the innkeeper please let them in?

The little boy who had rehearsed his lines so very carefully, listened patiently, and then said the seven words loud and clear: "There is no room in the inn."

Joseph turned, his shoulders sagging. But before he could leave, the innkeeper opened the door, thrust his head out, and said, loud and clear, "Wait...wait! You can have *my* room."

It wasn't in the script. Nor was it in the script on that first Christmas. *And so it was, that...she brought forth her firstborn son, and wrapped him in swaddling clothes, and laid him in a manger; because there was no room for them in the inn* (Luke 2:6,7).

As we recall this short resumé of the most beautiful story ever given from God, may your heart be reminded of the importance of remembering, not just the gifts that are to come, the families we are to see, and the loved ones we shall enjoy, but remembering the true message of Christmas—God's love for us. And may we not get so distracted by the many activities of the holiday season that we never even reach Bethlehem.

Dr. Van Impe and I are grateful for the opportunity to share the saving message of God's love for the world in these closing days of time. Thank you for your prayers and support.

Other Books
by Rexella Van Impe

Mirror, Mirror On the Wall, Who am I Fooling?

Who are you *really*—deep inside? Who do you see in your soul mirror? Discover how to let God live through you and make something beautiful of your life!

Satisfied...A Promise of Peace in a Troubled World

Is your life the way you want it to be? Do you face problems with depression, dissatisfaction, divorce, disaster, or deception? Rexella deals with these and other problems and offers practical, biblical guidance and advice.

The Tender Touch

In this intimate, heart-to-heart talk with women, Rexella discusses life, death, marriage, and family relationships. She shares deep insights gained through her personal experiences in ministry. Must reading for every Christian woman.

Hope and Fear Not
A revealing look through Mary and Joseph's eyes at the events surrounding the birth of Jesus. Feel the excitement and wonder they must have felt, and renew your desire to help proclaim God's message of hope for mankind.

Beware: Children in Peril
The horrible plague of child abuse touches every town, every neighborhood, in our nation. Rexella's carefully researched book destroys the myths about child abuse and suggests what can be done to stop this terrible disease and provide help and hope for its victims.

Encounters—Inspiration and Insight
We experience many "encounters" in life— some that change our whole lives. Are these "encounters" simply happenstances or does God direct our steps according to His purpose? Rexella shares "encounters" that will bless you and cause your faith to grow!

That Mystery Called Life
This book will stir you, challenge you, uplift you, encourage you, teach you, thrill you, and bless you. Its articles are intimate, moving, personal insights into the day-to-day reality of walking with the Lord!